Olympic Torch

vancouver 2010

Simon Rose

Weigl

Published by Weigl Educational Publishers Limited
6325 10th Street SE
Calgary, Alberta T2H 2Z9
Website: www.weigl.com

Library and Archives Canada Cataloguing in Publication

Rose, Simon, 1961-
          Canada's Olympic torch : Canadian icons / Simon Rose.
Includes index.
Also available in electronic format.
ISBN 978-1-77071-580-6 (bound).--ISBN 978-1-77071-587-5 (pbk.)
          1. Olympics--Social aspects--Canada--Juvenile literature. 2. Olympic
Torch Relay--Juvenile literture. I. Title.

GV721.92.R68 2010   j796.480971   C2010-903746-4

Printed in the United States of America in North Mankato, Minnesota
1 2 3 4 5 6 7 8 9 0 14 13 12 11 10

072010
WEP230610

Editor: Heather Kissock
Design: Terry Paulhus

Weigl acknowledges Getty Images and CP Images as image suppliers for this title.

Every reasonable effort has been made to trace ownership and to obtain permission to reprint copyright material. The publishers would be pleased to have any errors or omissions brought to their attention so that they may be corrected in subsequent printings.

We acknowledge the financial support of the Government of Canada through the Canada Book Fund for our publishing activities.

CONTENTS

4   What is an Olympic Torch?

7   The Story of the Torch

9   Making an Olympic Torch

10 Canada's Olympic Torches

13 The Flame Comes to Canada

14 The Torch Relay

16 The Torch's Journey

18 A Canadian Relay

20 Standing Guard at the Games

22 Make Your Own Olympic Torch

23 Find Out More

24 Glossary/Index

What is an Olympic Torch?

The Olympic flame and torch are two of the main **symbols** of the Olympics. The flame represents peace, hope, and **equality** for the whole world. It is lit before every Olympic and Paralympic Games at a ceremony held in Greece. The flame is then taken to the **host country**. There, it is used to light the Olympic torch during the opening ceremonies. The Olympic flame burns throughout the games. It is put out during the closing ceremonies.

The Story of the Torch

The first Olympic flame was lit in ancient Greece for the original Olympic Games. The flame first appeared at the modern Olympics in Amsterdam in 1928. It has been a **tradition** of the Olympics ever since.

In 1936, a new tradition began. The flame was transferred to a torch in the host country. People carried the torch across the country. This journey became known as the torch relay.

Making an Olympic Torch

A new torch is designed for every Olympics. The torch's design represents the host country and the **theme** of the games. The torch must not burn the people who will carry it. It also needs to be lightweight. Thousands of torches are made so that there are enough for the long torch relay.

Canada's Olympic Torches

The Olympic Games have been held in Canada three times. Montreal hosted the summer Olympics in 1976. Its torch looked like the torches used in ancient Greece. For the 1988 Winter Olympics in Calgary, the torch looked like the Calgary Tower.

The torch design for the Vancouver Winter Games in 2010 represented Canada's vast, open country. It also showed the lines winter sports, such as skiing and skating, make on snow and ice.

11

The Flame Comes to Canada

Vancouver, British Columbia, was the host city for the 2010 Winter Olympics. In October 2009, the Olympic flame was flown to British Columbia from Greece. To travel on the plane, the flame was put into six miner's lanterns.

The Torch Relay

The 2010 Olympic torch began in Victoria, British Columbia, on October 30, 2009. The torch was carried more than 45,000 kilometres over 106 days. This was the longest torch relay ever to take place within a host country. The Vancouver 2010 Olympic torch was carried by 12,000 people. It went to more than 1,000 Canadian communities. The torch travelled through every province and territory.

The Torch's Journey

Canadians use different types of **transportation**. Many of these forms of transportation were used during the Olympic torch relay. The torch travelled over land, air, and water. When the flame arrived in Victoria, it was carried across Victoria Harbour in a **First Nations** canoe. Other unique experiences took place once the relay began.

A Canadian Relay

Many people ran on foot with the torch. However, it was also carried in ways that were special to Canada. The torch travelled by dogsled, snowmobile, horse-drawn carriage, cross-country skis, kayak, tractor, mountain bike, surfboard, snowshoes, ferry, and plane.

Standing Guard at the Games

The torch's journey ended in Vancouver on February 12, 2010. The torch was used to light two Olympic **cauldrons**. One was at BC Place. This is where the opening ceremonies were held. The other cauldron was outdoors, on the Vancouver **waterfront**. The waterfront flame burned for the entire Winter Games. The flame was put out on February 28 at the closing ceremonies.

Make Your Own Olympic Torch

Supplies

1 sheet white
construction paper

clear tape

red, yellow, and
orange tissue paper

white glue

1. Roll the construction paper into a cone shape. Tape it closed.

2. Layer the tissue paper so that the red squares are on the bottom, the orange are in the middle, and the yellow are on top.

3. Gather the squares from the centre of the squares, and hold them in your hand like a bouquet of flowers.

4. Put some glue into the sides of the opening of the cone.

5. Press the tissue paper into the cone and let the glue dry.

6. Run your own Olympic relay in your yard or community with your friends.

Find Out More

To find out more about Canada's Olympic torch, visit these websites.

Vancouver 2010 Winter Olympics
www.vancouver2010.com

The Olympic Flame
http://entertainment.
howstuffworks.com/
olympic-torch.htm

**Enchanted Learning—
Olympics:**
www.enchanted
learning.com/olympics

The Olympic Movement
www.olympic.org

Glossary

cauldrons: large containers in which items are heated

equality: having the same rights and duties

First Nations: Canada's original inhabitants

host country: the place chosen for the Olympic Games

symbols: items meant to represent something

theme: the main idea of something

tradition: something that has been done in a certain way for a long time

transportation: ways of moving things from one place to another

waterfront: a part of a town or city than runs alongside a body of water

Index

design 9, 10

flame 4, 7, 9, 13, 20, 23

Greece 4, 7, 10, 13

Olympic Games 4, 7, 9, 10, 13, 23

opening ceremonies 4, 20

relay 7, 9, 14, 16, 18, 22

transportation 16

Vancouver 10, 13, 14, 20, 23